SCIENCE ACADEMY

BIG PUSH

BY KIRSTY HOLMES

CRABTREE
PUBLISHING COMPANY
WWW.CRABTREEBOOKS.COM

CRABTREE
PUBLISHING COMPANY
WWW.CRABTREEBOOKS.COM

Author:
Kirsty Holmes
Editorial director:
Kathy Middleton
Editors:
Madeline Tyler, Janine Deschenes
Proofreader:
Petrice Custance
Graphic design:
Ian McMullen
Prepress technician:
Katherine Berti
Print coordinator:
Katherine Berti

Library and Archives Canada Cataloguing in Publication

Title: Big push / by Kirsty Holmes.
Names: Holmes, Kirsty, author.
Description: Series statement: Science academy | Originally published: King's Lynn: BookLife, 2020. | Includes index.
Identifiers: Canadiana (print) 20200357786 | Canadiana (ebook) 20200357808 | ISBN 9781427130532 (hardcover) | ISBN 9781427130570 (softcover) | ISBN 9781427130617 (HTML)
Subjects: LCSH: Force and energy—Juvenile literature. | LCSH: Motion—Juvenile literature.
Classification: LCC QC73.4 .H652 2021 | DDC j531/.6—dc23

Library of Congress Cataloging-in-Publication Data

Names: Holmes, Kirsty, author.
Title: Big push / by Kirsty Holmes.
Description: New York : Crabtree Publishing Company, 2021. | Series: Big push | Includes index. | Audience: Ages 6-9 | Audience: Grades 2-3 | Summary: "The students of class 201 are locked out of their classroom. Professor Adams's car has broken down and they can't unlock the door without his nose print. Join the students of Science Academy as they learn how forces work and help Professor Adams get her car to move. Simple sentences and easy-to-understand examples make learning about forces understandable and fun"-- Provided by publisher.
Identifiers: LCCN 2020045824 (print) | LCCN 2020045825 (ebook) | ISBN 9781427130532 (hardcover) | ISBN 9781427130570 (paperback) | ISBN 9781427130617 (ebook)
Subjects: LCSH: Force and energy--Juvenile literature.
Classification: LCC QC73.4 .H653 2021 (print) | LCC QC73.4 (ebook) | DDC 531/.6--dc23
LC record available at https://lccn.loc.gov/2020045824
LC ebook record available at https://lccn.loc.gov/2020045825

Crabtree Publishing Company

www.crabtreebooks.com   1–800–387–7650
Published by Crabtree Publishing Company in 2021
© 2020 BookLife Publishing Ltd.

Published in Canada
Crabtree Publishing
616 Welland Ave.
St. Catharines, Ontario
L2M 5V6

Published in the United States
Crabtree Publishing
347 Fifth Ave
Suite 1402-145
New York, NY 10016

Printed in the U.S.A./122020/CG20201014

CONTENTS

Words that are bold, like **this**, can be found in the glossary on page 24.

ATTENDANCE

Another day at Science Academy has begun. Time to take attendance! Meet class 201.

Lewis

Favorite subject:
Electricity

Dee Dee

Favorite subject:
Movement

Katie

Favorite subject:
Pulling forces

Ling

Favorite subject:
Pushing forces

Paige

Favorite subject:
Magnets

Ravi

Favorite subject:
Energy

Today's lessons are all about forces called pushes. The students will learn answers to these questions:

- What is a force?
- What is a push?
- What are **contact** and noncontact forces?
- How can we use pushing forces?

Bud-E

Favorite subject:
Being helpful!

Science Academy is a school especially for kids who love science and solving problems! Do I hear the bell?

LOCKED CLASSROOM!

It's 9:00 a.m. at Science Academy. The morning bell has just rung. But the students in class 201 are not in their classroom. They're locked out!

Ouch! The bell is so loud! Why is the classroom locked? Where is Professor Adams?

The classroom doors at Science Academy are controlled by new noseprint **technology**. No one can get in without Professor Adams's noseprint. This is usually a good thing…but not today!

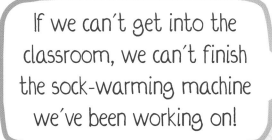

If we can't get into the classroom, we can't finish the sock-warming machine we've been working on!

Just then, Bud-E, the class robot, arrives. He found Professor Adams not far from the school. Her electric car ran out of power. She tried to push the car, but it would not move.

Professor Adams is just around the corner. She needs our help!

Bud-E tells the class that Professor Adams is not strong enough to push the car by herself. Now she will have to wait until a **tow truck** comes.

The tow truck won't get here for a few hours. Maybe I can find a way to push the car with the help of class 201 instead.

A PUSHING FORCE

The students run around the corner to find Professor Adams and her car. Professor Adams's car cannot move on its own. Its **electric motor** is broken. All objects, such as cars, need forces to make them move. A force is a push or pull that creates movement.

Pulling

Pushing

I have tried a few types of forces to make my car move.

Kicking [A kick is a type of push.]

Professor Adams explains that she needs a big push to move the car. A push is a force. It moves an object away from you. A push can also make a moving object move faster.

The harder we push, the faster you go!

LUNCHTIME

The pushing has been tiring! The classmates head back to school for lunch. As they eat, they look around for other types of forces. Paige picks up a magnet. It pulls an **iron** nail toward it! She tells her classmates that a magnet uses a noncontact force to pull the nail.

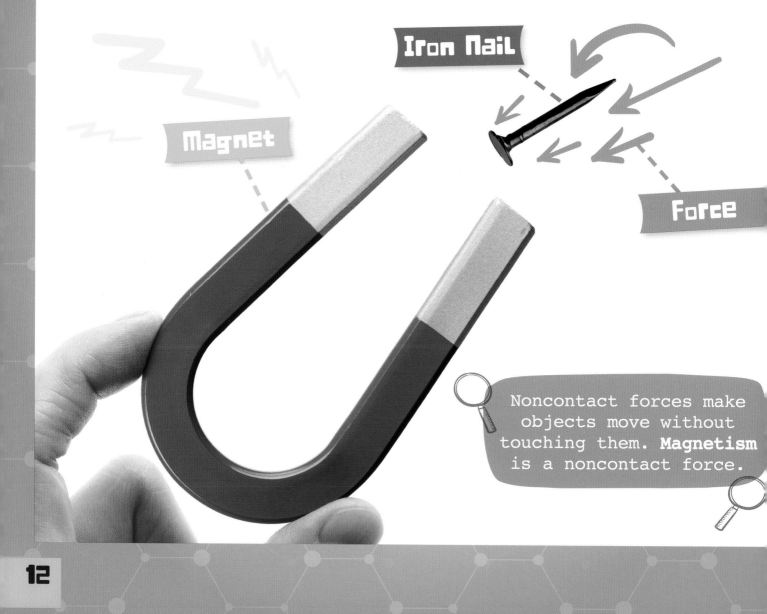

Iron Nail

Magnet

Force

Noncontact forces make objects move without touching them. **Magnetism** is a noncontact force.

Ling explains that a push is a different kind of force. It is a contact force. Contact forces touch objects to make them move. Professor Adams put her hands on the car and pushed to make it move.

I pushed my chair toward my desk to clean up after lunch. Then, I pushed open the door to go outside for recess! Each time, I put my hands on the object to make it move.

A big push is needed to move a heavy object, such as Professor Adams's car. A big push can also make a light object move farther or faster. A kick is a push. With a big kick, Ling can move the soccer ball across the whole field!

Small force

Large force

A small push can move a light object. You can easily push a toy car with your hand or push air out of your mouth when you blow out candles. Look at the objects below. Do they need big or small pushes?

Baseball

Shopping cart

Buttons on a remote

Swing

MORE FORCE NEEDED!

Ling explains that the car is too heavy for Professor Adams to push on her own. The students of class 201 try to help Professor Adams push the car. But it is still too heavy.

The car will not move without a bigger force. We need a really, really big push!

Suddenly, Ravi points at something down the street. A huge robot is walking toward them! It looks very strong. The ground shakes with each step it takes. Ling is excited. Maybe the robot can give the car a huge push!

Hello, **puny** humans! I am Res-Q, your friendly neighborhood rescue robot. How can I help?

Res-Q gives a big push…and the car moves! Res-Q is very strong and even heavier than the car. This lets the robot push with a lot of force. Res-Q pushes the car all the way to school.

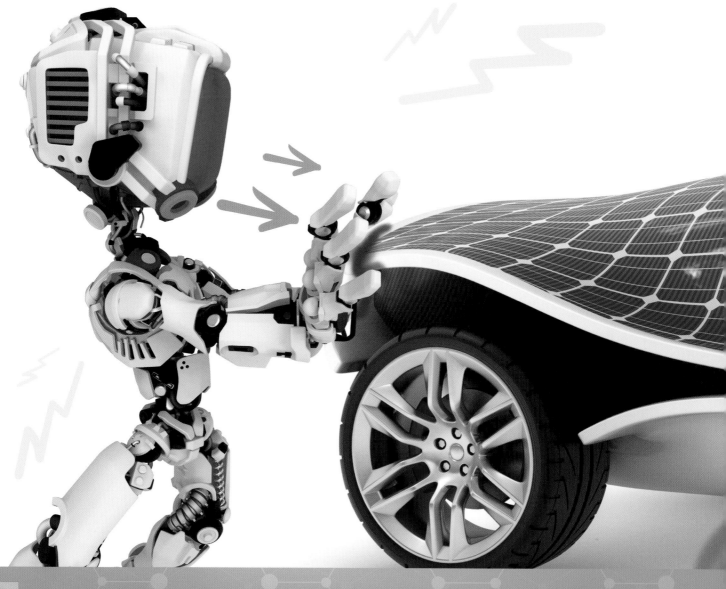

Professor Adams is so happy! Class 201 is happy, too. They have learned a lot about pushing forces. Professor Adams looks at the clock. The bell is about to ring. The students will have to finish the sock-warming machine tomorrow.

All in a day's work, Professor Adams.

Thanks for the big push, Res-Q!

ALL KINDS OF PUSH FORCES

People use many kinds of pushing forces. Kicking, throwing, and blowing are all types of pushing forces. Do you use pushing forces in any other ways?

Pushing down on the pedals makes the bicycle move.

Pushing the switch turns on the light.

The wind pushes this pinwheel, making it turn.

Throwing a ball is a push that moves the ball away from you.

Pushing a snow shovel makes the snow move across the ground.

PROBLEM SOLVED

The bell rings and the school day is over.
Professor Adams says goodbye to the class.

Thanks for your help today, everyone!
Now...how will I get home? Res-Q, can
you push my car to a repair shop?

HOMEWORK

Can you find all the science words in this word search?

C	O	N	T	A	C	T	E
A	B	D	W	P	X	I	K
Y	U	C	P	Q	K	O	R
I	N	R	A	D	I	P	F
P	U	S	H	R	C	P	O
E	C	J	H	W	K	Z	R
M	A	B	L	O	P	Q	C
P	M	A	G	N	E	T	E

1. Contact
2. Kick
3. Push

4. Car
5. Magnet
6. Force

GLOSSARY

CONTACT	Touch
ELECTRIC MOTOR	A machine that turns electrical energy into movement
FORCE	A push or pull that creates movement
IRON	A strong, hard metal
MAGNETISM	The pulling force of a magnet
PUNY	Small or weak
TECHNOLOGY	The use of science and engineering to solve problems and complete tasks
TOW TRUCK	A truck with special equipment that allows it to pull other vehicles

INDEX